AF366462

PIERRE ALEXANDRE
GEORGET

John Lennon: A Life to Live

Theatre Play

Presentation

The genesis of this play is the reading of a book, a "big" book...

I originally read Lesley-Ann Jones' book[1] as a novel. I loved the vivid, researched writing. Then, rather than taking notes as I read, the idea came to me to write a play that would focus on John's youth and adolescence, without too much emphasis on the Beatles themselves. Rather, it would highlight the personality and character traits and facts that marked his life, forged his success and at the same time explain (or highlight) the character John Lennon himself, from his Liverpudlian "origins" to his death in New York.

This book is not a biography, far from it. It is a work of fiction. I have tried to bring John Lennon to life, or to relive him, with what has been told. It takes elements (only passages) from the life of the rock-pop star and adapts them to the stage.
It shows characters from John's entourage or his relatives, but also purely invented beings to underline one character trait or another.
The dialogues are imaginary. However, each one reflects a portion of reality according to the information gathered: it is up to the reader to sort it out.

---

[1] Lesley-Ann Jones / "What Killed John Lennon - Lives and Deaths of a Legend" published by ALISIO in 2020 (Original title: "Who Killed John Lennon" / John Blake Publishing - Bonnier Books UK / 2020)

To adopt an idea from the author, I did not want to disappoint his fans or discredit the world star that he was. Simply to raise certain aspects and highlight them.
I have done a lot of research to make the events seem real, while respecting what the genius singer-songwriter experienced. I wanted to stay as close to reality as possible. However, the acts are animated by fantasy and the desire to entertain but also to open doors away from hackneyed or hackneyed ideas and to ask questions.
For the rest, everything is an invention of the author.

The author and the actors wish you a great time! "A splendid time is guaranteed for all[2]"!

---

[2] Being For The Benefit Of Mr. Kite! song.

Introduction

John Lennon certainly did not have an easy life, contrary to what his success might suggest.
His life has not been the "long, quiet river" as each of us would have liked.

This play reveals John's attachment to his family and friends; his connection with a "group".
To quote Richard Hughes in Lesley-Ann Jones' extraordinarily fascinating book: "Narcissists are often fusional. [Lennon] was idealising. He needed a 'twin', a mirror. I think of his relationships that mattered... where does one begin and the other does end? ".

This play highlights the difficulties, the wanderings, the successes and the questions of the great creator that he was. Eccentric, he was also a committed singer, who became more and more so in the course of his life and according to his encounters, notably with his last wife.
Sometimes egocentric, often immensely generous in his imagination, his sources of inspiration and his work, his life can be summed up in one thing:
"A Life to live", and we would probably all have liked to live it...

Being creative is about fighting against what puts you down. Show and prove that you exist. Nothing will be able to resist you until you have achieved your goal: to bring forth, to create to exist.

Lennon is undoubtedly a victim of the double-belonging or double-abandonment complex: did my father abandon me because he is a sailor or because my mother cheats on him? Did my mother abandon me because she is frivolous and becomes indulgent when she takes me in?
It is from this latent double anxiety that John's complex and anguished personality was born.

John Lennon, like Mark Chapman his murderer, J.D. Salinger, the author of "The Catcher in the Rye" and his protagonist Holden Caulfield, are all 'fatherless' boys, having had a literally 'absent' father.
Men who have not had life explained to them always take refuge in something.
For some, they become self-taught, believing in their destiny and in their lucky star.
The famous Canadian and Jungian psychotherapist Guy Corneau speaks of "Missing father, missing son" in his famous book, having himself been confronted with the first mass murder in history, in a school in Canada by a boy with an absent father.
Something to think about.

John Lennon : A Life to Live

The Characters

In order of appearance on stage:

1. John Lennon – Musician, composer and singer
2. Stuart Sutcliffe (aka Stue) - Artist, friend of John and bassist of the Quarry Men
3. Julia Lennon - John's mother
4. Alfred Lennon (known as Alf) - John's father
5. Billy Hall - (voice) Alf's colleague
6. Pete Shotton (aka Snowball) - John's childhood friend. Played washboard in the seminal band The Quarry Men.
7. Nigel Walley - (voice) Friend of John, present at the accident.
8. Police officer - On the scene of the accident
9. Eric Plague - The driver responsible for the accident, an off-duty police officer.
10. Pete Best, son of Mona Best, patron of the Casbah in Liverpool, drummer, friend of John.
11. Klaus Voormann, German artist, friend of the Beatles and of John.
12. St Peter's Parish Priest: welcomes the Fab Four.
13. George, figuratively present.
14. Paul, figuratively present.
15. Ringo, figuratively present.

16.   Elvis Presley, the American Rock and Roll idol, admired by John.
17.   Sigmund Freud, the famous psychotherapist.
18.   Johnny Hallyday, French singer, idol of the youth.
19.   Inspector Cox of the New York FBI.
20.   Agent Dipps of the New York FBI.
21.   Mark David Chapman, John Lennon's killer.
22.   Jerome David Salinger, American writer, author of the novel 'The Catcher in the Rye', which Chapman is said to have based on.
23.   The Policeman, Chapman's interrogator.
24.   The Doctor: John's psychoanalyst reappears.

Scene 1 - Liverpool

Liverpool and the harbour after the Second World War bombings.
When the curtain opens, the stage is in darkness.
Some photos (or films) appear in the background on a video screen.

Scene 2 - Stue

Light. A wasteland.
When the scene lights up, a pile of bricks is visible. A teenager is sitting on it. It is John. He is a teenager, probably about fifteen years old. He is wearing a bright checked shirt and the old gabardine that belonged to his Uncle George. He is scribbling in a sketchbook.
Stue comes to meet him. Stuart Sutcliffe is a Scottish art student that will play bass in the band.

Stue   (he arrives) Hi!

John   Hi. (He puts his sketchbook down beside him).

Stue   How are you?

John   I'm ok.

Stue   Don't you go to school?

John   No.

Stue   What are you doing?

John   Nothing. I'm just goofing off!

Stue   (in today's style) What's your name?

John   John Lennon. What about you?

Stue   I'm Stue, Stuart Sutcliffe. Don't you go to
          Quarry Bank Grammar School here in
          Liverpool?

John   Yes, I do.

Stue   The same school as me!

John   I haven't seen you yet!

Stue   Well, I don't often go...

John   Me not either... After this, my Aunt would like
          me to go to Liverpool College of Art.

Stue   Do you live with her?

John   Yes.

Stue   All the time?

John   Yes.

Stue   What about your mother's house?

John   She lives with another guy.

Stue   (showing a sketchbook at his feet) Is this yours?

John   Well, yes.

Stue   Let me see!

John   (hands him the sketchbook) Here!

Stue   (consulting the notebook) Wow, that's trash!

John   Do you think so?

Stue   Well, yes! A singer with four eyes...a hunchback full of warts...

John   (a little aggressive) No problem! If you don't like it, you don't have to look! (He reaches for his notebook).

Stue   Well, that's fine, I was just saying that; I like it. (He gives him back the notebook).

John   Thank you!

Stue   Where did you learn?

John   Nowhere. I draw with Julia.

Stue   Who is she?

John   Julia? My mother. I go over to her house every
          now and then. She's fun. She teaches me.

Stue   And that's it?

John   No. I also play music!

Stue   What do you play?

John   Skiffle.

Stue   Everyone plays that music around here, in
          Mendips or Liverpool. It's very trendy!

John   So what? I like it!

Stue   This is old music, pal, folk music!

John   ...but it's in the air now, and there are jazz
          chords. You can arrange it.

Stue   How did you learn?

John   With Julia.

Stue   Also?

John   Also! She taught me the banjo. And my father,
          the harmonica.

Stue   What does your father do?

John   He is a sailor.

Stue   What's his name?

John   Alfred, or Freddie, but everyone calls him Alf.

Stue   … "Alf the sailor"! That does it!

John   Yeah! (Silence).

Stue   Play! (He noticed a harmonica sticking out of John's shirt pocket).

John   Play what?

Stue   Well, the music.

John   I'm not in the mood!

Stue   Come on!

John   (He takes his harmonica out of his pocket. He starts the intro of "Love Me Do" on a Horner harmonica).

Stue   Great!

John   Do you like it?

Stue   Yes, really!

John   Well, that's good then. Because we're looking for a musician; a bass player.

Stue   Really? Look, it could be done, we'll have to see. Do you have a band? Are you with friends?

John   Yes.

Stue   What is the name?

John   Pete (Snowball Shotton), Len Garry, Eric Griffiths, Rod Davis and Colin Hanton.

Stue   No, your Group?

John   The Quarry Men.

Stue   Same as school actually!

John   Yes.

Stue   Are you playing me something again?

John   No, I don't have time... I have to go.

Stue   Where?

John   At my mother's house in Allerton. Then I go home to Mendips to my Aunt.

Stue   What is your aunt's name?

John   ...you, you like to know everything! Mimi! That's her name. It's Mary. Mary Stanley.

Stue   Okay. See you at school then?

John   Maybe, or if not, here.

Stue   Right. (He hesitates) Because I also draw...

John   (bossy and fatherly at the same time) Show it to me when you get a chance.

They both stand up and disappear to one side of the stage. The lights are turned off.

Scene 3 - Julia's flat

In Julia's flat in Allerton. Clutter everywhere, a basic décor. A banjo in one corner, an acoustic guitar in the other. John and Julia are sitting on footstools.

Julia   What's the matter, John? You look so idle, so dejected.

John   Why don't we see Dad more often?

Julia   I've already explained to you that your father and I are separated.

John   So what?

Julia   And then, I told you, he's a sailor. He's always at sea; he sails on big ships across the oceans of the globe; he travels the seas of the five continents.

John   (silence).

Julia   (as if to justify herself) That's why we don't see him often!

John   He was teaching me stuff, he plays the harmonica, he sings.

Julia   Yes, I know, you miss him a lot.

John   Not just me, I hope?

Julia   No, me too. And then there are other problems...

John   Which ones?

Julia   He drinks. You know, sailors drink a lot. And he gets into fights.

John   (getting angry, in denial) Shut up! You're saying that because you're angry with him. It's not my problem. I don't want to hear it! (Then, louder) He's my father!

Julia   I know, it's very important to you; I'm sorry.

John   You don't give a shit! That's why you're living with that new guy, that John Dykins, that guy with the same name as me, that's why you even call him Bobby. Because of that, because of him and because of you, Mimi put us on welfare, and I had to go and live with her.

Julia   Yes, I like it better if you say that it was she who ratted us out, as you say.

John   Why?

Julia   Because I was afraid that you would think it was me, that I didn't want you anymore.

John   It's all the same. I'm being tossed around, I don't know where to go. Nobody wants me anymore!

Julia   But I do. (She approaches, he pushes her away). And then you have Mimi. She's your Aunt!

John   You can talk about it! She's as annoying as the drizzle and she's always annoying me. (He mimes) "Where have you been? Have you been doing your homework? Why aren't you working?".

Julia   She says that for your own good.

John   You bet! (He mimes again) "And your mates! Little Pete Snowball Shotton, that blond kid. What a bum! Just like the rest of them! They're all thugs".

Julia   (sorry) But you have Uncle George too, don't you? You like him and he likes you.

John   Yeah, at least he cares about me a little bit. (Reflecting) Otherwise, I don't exist. (Raising his voice) For nobody! No one! I don't exist for anyone!

Julia   (after a while) Come on! Calm down. Come on, let's play the banjo. I gave it to you specifically for the school festival and "your" (she insists) concert. The concert with your band, the Quarry Men.

John   (seems to have calmed down).

Julia   You're going to get on a truck, imagine that! All your mates on that truck laughing...sorry, playing Skiffle and singing. I can see you from here! And everyone looking at you.

John   Yeah, that could be cool!

Julia   Top, you mean! You're going to play the songs "Puttin' on the Style" and "Baby Let's Play House" in a very original way. I like the idea.

John   Me too, I confess.

Julia   And Pete, contrary to what Aunt Mimi says, with his washboard, he is too original!

John   He's not the only musician!

Julia   I know. We'll see you too, of course. And then, you're the one who sings!

John   (seeking a compliment) Yes, all in all, not too great!

Julia   Yes, it is! Only, we still have to rehearse. A lot of rehearsing. You know that. It's not easy to do if you want to be successful.

John   (this line from his mother seemed to please John who said nothing more).

Scene 4 - John's abduction

Muted music: Drunken Sailor by The Irish Rovers or by Ferre Grignard

A 'ghostly' appearance of Alf (Freddie), John's Father, dressed as a sailor, walking towards the doorway (at the home of Billy Hall, a colleague, in Blackpool), a light on his back (a bit like Mozart's Requiem).

The mother rings the doorbell. She comes to see Alf, who has taken refuge with John in Blackpool, to negotiate: she wants to take her son back with her to drop him off at Aunt Mimi's. Alf wants to go to New Zealand with John. Dialogue and negotiation between the father and mother.

Julia   Can I come in?

Alf   Come on in!

They enter a very British style lounge.

Julia   (silent)

Alf   Sit down.

Julia   Thank you. (They sit down)

Alf   I didn't expect you here in Blackpool. For a surprise...

Julia   I heard that you came here to take refuge with your friend, Billy Hall.

Alf   (softly) Take refuge, take refuge... (Silence)

Julia   I went yesterday to Aunt Mimi and Uncle George's, who look after John. They told me that you came to see them...

Alf   Mmm mmm!

Julia   ...to take John shopping with you. (Then, with a reproachful tone) For once!

Alf   Well, yes.

Julia   (raising her voice slightly) The problem is that you didn't do it! Instead, you came here with John to your friend's house.

John is in the corner, listening without batting an eyelid.

Alf   Yes.

Julia   Without really warning and saying where you were going.

Alf   (silence)

Julia   Mimi and Uncle George were worried. They warned me. So I came as fast as I could. I knew you'd be here.

Alf   Yes, well. And then?

Julia   I guess if you did it, you have intentions?

Alf   Yes, I'm actually moving to New Zealand. And I'd like to take John with me, to look after him... That way, you wouldn't have to do it anymore! I'll be with him all the time.

Julia   Okay... (In a tone of surprise and disapproval)

Alf   I've been thinking about this for a long time and wanted to do this.

Julia   Mmm mmm!

Alf   To stay with George and Mimi, it's not right. It's not right, for him, I mean. I mean, I...

Julia   Yes, but it's a decision. And it's best to stick to it.

Alf   (vague) Maybe.

Julia   If you want to think about the child's balance.

Alf   Yes, but with your new boyfriend, you're in no condition to... (Then he changes his mind, wanting to calm things down, and interrupts himself)

Julia   Look, I think it's better, (Rephrases) it's more reasonable that he comes back with me. That way, things will go back to normal, (Insinuating) and we won't have to talk about "kidnapping" and all.

Alf   That was not my intention.

Julia   I agree, but it could look like this...

Alf   I thought I was doing it for him, for his balance, for his good.

Julia   (she wants to say, now you're thinking about it, but changes her mind) Imagine how complicated it is! Following his father to the other side of the world. A deep-sea sailor. Professional. He's still young.

Alf   I know.

Julia   He has his habits in England. His studies, his
         friends.

Alf   I just wanted to help him.

Julia   Of course, I'm convinced that he realizes this;
         that he appreciates your approach and your
         intention.

Alf   I would like him to come with me, I would like
         to be with him. (Turning awkwardly to John)
         John, what do you think?

Julia   Alf, please!

Alf   What do you say, John? You want to be with
         your dad, don't you?

John   (softly) I will.

Alf   We will leave tomorrow then. It will be a great
         journey.

Julia   (knowing full well what she's going to do) Well,
         if that's the way it is, I'm off. (She stands up).

John   Mum! (He runs to her and takes refuge in her
         arms).

Alf   (after a moment, to his wife) Listen, stay calm
           for a while.

Julia   (she calms down).

Alf   What can we do then?

Julia   I think it's clear. Let's both be reasonable. He
           can't be at my place, because of the situation you
           know (She refers to the presence of her new
           boyfriend), nor can he be with you, because of
           your situation too. You are never there, that's
           your real job. You travel all the time. Sometimes
           (referring to drinking) you capsize too...

Alf   (he smiles and is silent).

Julia   At other times, you live the life of a true
           adventurer. You enjoy it. You smuggle some
           goods. You do a little business on the side, like
           many of our sailors. You make ends meet with
           your little traffic. The coastguards know about
           it, they have you in their sights, but you deftly
           slip through the net, as you are used to. You're
           doing a good job of it: your little alcohol and
           cigarette business is flourishing.

Alf   (he smiles again).

Julia   All this is unfortunately far from the concerns of
           a child or a young teenager. Your world of sailor
           and schemes is another world, a hundred miles

away from his world. How can you take care of
him in these conditions? It's impossible.

Alf   (dropping his guard) I know.

Julia   That's why he won't (she insists) go with me or
          with you. That's the way it is. (Let it Be). I'm
          taking him with me. We go to the station. He's
          going back to Uncle George and Aunt Mimi. It's
          getting better all the time.

Alf   (scowling) OK, that's fine. Take him. And then
          go away!

Julia   Don't be upset, he won't be with me either.

Alf   That's fine. Farewell! Goodbye John!

John   (not responding).

They put on their coats and walk out the door without
saying anything more.

Alf   (in a casual tone, to them) The matter is closed!
          (Then calling his friend) Billy! Bring a bottle!

Billy   (voice) Here it comes!

Alf   Now that they're gone for good, let's get drunk!

Music: Drunken Sailor - Ferre Grignard
Curtain time for a change of scenery.

A phantasmagorical vision: father and son, in the style of Captain Hook versus Peter Pan.
Is John dreaming?
They are on the deck of a ship in a storm.
The storm symbolises an inner storm between father and son: you have abandoned me!
They hang from the shrouds and talk face to face in the sound of the wind and the fury of the roaring sea.
They speak loudly.

Alf   (thinking he recognises Peter Pan) Peter!

John   I am not Peter Pan!

Alf   Who are you?

John   I am John.

Alf   Where are you from?

John   I'm from another ship. Looking for you! And you're not Captain Hook.

Alf   Who do you think I am then?

John   You are Alf!

Alf   You, "little one", are nothing but a vulgar crewman, a ship's boy.

John   Speak for yourself!

Alf   I'm a captain!

John   My eye! You are nothing. You're just a sailor! A steward.

Alf   I don't even know you!

John   I know that. You abandoned me...

Alf   I've left.

John   But I've come to find you now, where you're hiding!

Alf   Leave me alone!

John   You are a coward, a scoundrel!

Alf   I went on an adventure, to travel the seas and oceans of the globe to feed you. I sailed, even in the Mediterranean sea, to Algeria.

John   I don't care! All I know is that you weren't there when I needed you.

Alf   I'm a hero, mate. I was on the North Atlantic convoys to supply our country England during the War.

John   Don't mind.

Alf   I was sailing, my friend, I was sailing...

John   Maybe, but in the process of sailing, you've become detached from me.

Alf   Goddam!

John   And finally, you never came back. I felt lost, forsaken. Abandoned.

Alf   It's not true! With and the flow, the tide, the surf of the sea carrying me, I come back and reappear every time.

John   Lies! You are never there.

Alf   It's my job, I can't do otherwise. We are sailors from father to son; your grandfather was a sailor too.

John   Pretext or excuse!

Alf   You're here to settle a score.

John   Now is the time to do it.

Alf   So never! Your mum doesn't want me anyway. She lives with a bloke, that "Bobby". Before that, she cheated on me with a Welsh, that

Taffy. So, for me, when it's like that, I just leave. I get the hell out of there.

John   It's easy!

Alf   Happy to be on this ship, I embark, I raise the mooring, I sail far away, on the enchanted Seas towards other skies and lost Paradises.

John   You are not Hook and you are not going to the island of Neverland!

Alf   (as if he hadn't heard anything) ...And I eat the delicious Scouse (sailor's stew) prepared by the cook on board. Then I lie down on my hammock without thinking about anything else, to escape and dream. I never get to the end of this journey...

John   I wanted you to teach me things, to play the harmonica. But you weren't there. You never came.

Alf   ...When I feel like it, I go up on deck and smoke a Pall Mall at my leisure; I watch the gulls and the foam on the sea; "I let the wind bathe my naked head"[3].

John   Fed up! Sadness. Disgust.

---

[3] Inspired by Verlaine

Alf   I know. One day I'll come back. And I'll take you far, far away with me. Just the two of us, to New Zealand for example.

John   Nonsense! You're nothing but a buccaneer, a smuggler, a privateer. Not even a captain!

Alf   I'll show you who I am, everything I can do...and we'll be happy, you'll see.

John   Nonsense. You forget me...

At that moment, John screams. A wave sweeps him away, and Father is left alone on his ship. Distraught.
The lights go out and the noise stops just as suddenly. Silence.

Scene 6 - Pete Shotton and John at school

Pete Snowball Shotton - the sowing wild oats accomplice who plays washboard in the Group.

The scene represents a school class.
Two characters are sitting on a bench, the teacher facing them. One of them is blond haired.
You can imagine as many extras as you like; they will then react loudly to John's impertinent remarks!
The teacher should use derision and a lot of humour, in the second degree.
He continually attacks both of them, especially John.

The Professor   (handing out a copy of John's student newspaper) Dear Mr Lennon, I see you've done it again! (Then turning to Pete Shotton) Same to you, Mr Shotton!

John   Sir, this is just a student newspaper!

The Professor   Yes, okay, but to caricature your teachers and the management to such an extent!

John   Sir, I assure you, it's not your nose!

The Professor   Is that so?

John   Yours doesn't have all those big buttons!

(His accomplice laughs)

The Professor   And what's more, you're entertaining the gallery!

John   It's better than falling asleep in your class, sir!

Here we can project a view of the cover of John's diary.

The Professor   "The Daily Howl"! You are playing with words, Mr Lennon: the scream, the owl. The howl with an "h"! The night owl is you, isn't it?

John   Sir, I can't go out at night. Aunt Mimi doesn't allow it.

The Professor   That's good! She's right. That way she won't complain about you smoking outside. Is this cry of your newspaper a cry of distress or of protest?

John   It's for fun.

The Professor   I see. That's all you know how to do! And your little friend there, next to you, the same thing! Right, Mr Shotton?

Shotton   (he doesn't flinch)

The Professor   We have fun, we have fun... You're right! Like when you threw all the sponges in the class out of the window. I'll tell your Aunt about it when she comes.

John   I don't care, she never agrees anyway.

The Professor   Like when you sneak off to see the girls at Strawberry Fields[4]. Your Auntie Mimi herself made it clear that if you did it again, she would hang you!

---

[4] This inspired the song.

Music 'Strawberry Fields For Ever' (extract).

John	We're not doing anything wrong!
The Professor	Is that true, Mr Shotton?
Pete	Yes, sir, that's right.
The Professor	And you, Mr Shotton, your little friends, why do they call you "Snowball"?
Pete	Because of the colour of my hair, Sir (He's blond).
The Professor	Are you in Mr Lennon's Group?
Pete	Yes.
The Professor	And what do you play?
Pete	Washboard.
The Professor	Is that so? Are you doing the laundry?
Pete	No, it's a musical instrument.
The Professor	And Mr. Lennon, what does he play?
Pete	Guitar. And he sings.
The Professor	I see. It must be beautiful!

| Pete | (ironically to John) Besides, he plays very well, you know, sir! |

| John | (resentful, to Pete) You, watch out at break time!
(To the teacher) You can come and listen to us at the school party. |

| The Professor | I will come. Now, let's get back to our class. I'm going to give you a book to read, which was written by an American just after the war. |

| Pete | (interrupts). Did you make War, sir? |

| The Professor | Yes, Mr Shotton. I "made" it, as you say. And I even met this writer quite by chance when I landed with him on the beaches of Normandy. |

| John | What is his name (Interested in books)? |

| The Professor | Salinger. And his novel is The Catcher in The Rye. You go and get it from the library. In America, they read it a lot and it's recommended by the schools[5]. |

| John | America is not us! |

| The Professor | Mr. Lennon, please don't keep replying. |

---

[5] Strangely enough, this book has been a great success in the United States and has been a reference in schools.

A stern figure with a cane in his hand enters.

The Professor   Oh , by the way, here's the Director coming to reprimand you again. I think you've done it again!

The Director   Mr Lennon, come here.

John   (gets up) No, not with that, you can't!

The Director   Where do you think we are, Mr Lennon?

John   In England.

The Director   Put your hands (he wants to say "your dirty hands", but he knows how to keep his composure and phlegm) on the desk.

John   (he does so, with his back and buttocks facing the class).

The Director   (he hits the cane on the trousers several times).

John   (doesn't flinch, but you can see the revolt on his face).

The Director   Return to your seat.

John   I can't sit down anymore!

The Director   Well, then stay up! Next! (No one moves). Mr Shotton!

Pete   (gets up, and suffers the same fate; but he shouts).

The Director   In your place.

Pete   (sits down painfully).

The Director   The next time you misbehave, I'll have you both expelled. (He leaves the classroom with his cane in his hand).

John   Fed up with this shop!

The Professor   (insidious) There is nothing holding you back, Mr Lennon, you have understood that. I'm waiting for your Aunt to come and tell her about your behaviour. As for you, you can leave. You still have work to do in the study room.

John   Bastard   !

The Professor   (he gets angry and raises his voice) Take the opportunity to review your dishevelled style, your Aunt is coming!

And your insults won't change anything! Get out!

John   (gets up and walks out. He slams the door ostensibly).

The end-of-course bell is heard.

The Professor   You can go, I'll welcome Mrs Smith.

The class gets up and leaves. The last one closes the door.

The Professor   (he goes to the door and opens it to let Aunt Mimi through).

The Professor   Please, Madam, sit down. I thank you for coming, because the situation is rather serious for John. As you have no doubt heard about it, he is at the bottom of his class and it is getting worse.
All the teachers, and I'm not the only one, complain about his attitude and behaviour.
First of all, with regard to his friends: he fights and thinks he is the kingpin.
In class, he heckles the class and disturbs the other students.
Then he interrupts the teachers, disrupts the class and he is disobliging.
In addition to drawing his friend Pete Shotton into dangerous situations, I now learn that he writes and distributes

scribblings, obscene drawings to say the least, and writes mindless poems.

The Aunt	(listens carefully without saying anything).

The Professor	(he continues) Listen to this, I'm reading from his poem "Sad Michael[6]" (he reads): "He'd had a 'hard day's night' that day, for Michael was a cocky Watchtower. "A hard day's night", Madam, think about it! A hard day's night, or a night of a hard day! It doesn't make sense! A hard day's work, (he repeats) go figure, because this character Sad Michael sells books that he hijacks by pretending to be deaf and dumb! (He laughs).

The Aunt	But he's got a quirky sense of humour and he likes puns. John's got a sense of humour, you know. He's human, he's resentful. He's willing to be provocative to get people interested in him. He's self-taught, he learns on his own, with assistance sometimes: it suits him better.

The Professor	Yes, perhaps, but derision is not the "nonsense" that is so much vaunted but which leads to absurdity and

---

[6] From John Lennon's book of poems: 'In His Own Write' / 'En Flagrant Délire'.

nonsense. His English teacher will tell you about it: personally, my colleague appreciates it less! In fact, we're talking about throwing John out of our school. The best way to calm him down would be, believe me, to enrol him in another school, Madam, in an art school.

The Aunt   I am well aware, Professor, but there is nothing I can do! John is estranged from his parents; he feels abandoned and very frustrated about it all. I do what I can, but he doesn't want to hear it. He is only interested in music!

The Teacher   Yes, but at school, apart from the end-of-year party, we don't just play music!

The Aunt   I know. I keep telling him. Besides, I told him that he would never make a living with music[7]!

The Professor   Surely.

The Aunt   But he's puting everything into it; what do you want? Fortunately music is there, it's his outlet. Music is his whole life!

The Professor   No doubt, no doubt. Right. Good. (He stands up and shakes her hand). Thank you for coming.

---

[7] Authentic sentence.

The accident. The death of John's mother, Julia, in front of John's friend Nigel Walley.
Tyre squeals, dialogue, slamming doors, sirens…
The mother is no more.

Julia

(coming out of her sister Mimi's who lives in Menlove Avenue). (Julia's voice) Hi Nigel, what are you doing at Auntie Mimi's?

Nigel Walley

(voice) Hi, Julia. I'm here to see John, but Mimi says he's not in. I'll be back. See ya! (Presumably he's walking away)...

Screeching tyres. Shock.

Nigel Walley   (voices) Julia! No! Help!

Sirens. Slamming doors.

Police officer

(arrived on the scene) Who are you, what happened?

Eric Plague

(the driver responsible for the accident, an off-duty police officer) I am the driver. I am a police officer. I didn't see her coming! I couldn't stop in time! I'm sorry...

Police officer   Have you been drinking?

End of Scene

Scene 8 - Stue 2

Return from the School Party. They meet again.

Stue   It was a good party in the Rose Queen Garden at St Peter's Church!

John   Yeah, afterwards we even went through the cemetery! A bit of an iconoclast! (He thinks of Eleanor Rigby[8]).

Stue   Andon that truck, you were great!

John   Thank you.

Stue   I heard that you took Paul into your Group, following a long discussion after your concert?

John   Yes, it is.

Stue   He's not from this school, is he?

---

[8] The grave that inspired the song.

John   No, he goes to the Liverpool Institute.

Stue   More of a snob!

John   If you like, but I don't mind. It can bring in another audience to us.

Stue   A pretty good guy by the looks of it.

John   (this is the beginning of an emulation that already irritates John. But John needs him) I confess. He can play several instruments! He plays guitar, bass and drums when he has to; piano too. He's left-handed. And quite talented, I must say. He sings: we can do duets and backing vocals. We compose together and it works well.

Stue   He...

John   Otherwise, have you thought about it?

Stue   About what?

John   To join the Group.

Stue   I can't play.

John   But you draw, I learned. And much better than me!

Stue   You are exaggerating.

John   Yes, and I know you've already sold even!

Stue   It's a start.

John   My drawings, by comparison, are just silhouettes, caricatures.

Stue   Yes, but I like your writing in the school magazine "The Daily Howl". It rocks!

John   Yes, I'm not shy with my puns, my absurd poems and my caricatures. Everyone gets a kick out of it, have you seen how I make fun of teachers, in particular?

Stue   Yes.

John   So what do you decide?

Stue   I'm not sure.

John   Look, I'm telling you a secret, but you can't tell anyone, just between us, okay?

Stue   Ok.

John   Swear to it!

Stue   Cross my heart and hope to die!

John   Okay. I need your help. We get along well, we both draw. We might even crash at a flat together one day.

Stue   Yes.

John   Okay. But you have to keep the new kid in check, you know?

Stue   Yes.

John   Everybody needs everybody. I need a good one! And one who plays well.

Stue   So not me!

John   Yeah, but on the other hand, to compensate, I need someone to support me and listen to me. A real buddy! You know what I mean?

Stue   Yes.

John   In exchange, I promise to push you to the audition.

Stue   What if I don't pass the test?

John   Never mind, I'll do it. And you will be able to say "I hope we passed the audition"!

Stue   In the end, you are a bit like your father.

John   What do you mean by that?

Stue   A bit of a trickster, a fixer, a calculator. Successful in his little schemes and tricks...

John   Maybe, but that's how it is if you want to be the leader of a Group and stay that way! If you don't want to get screwed.

Stue   And what do you actually play?

John   Harmonica,

Stue   Banjo?

John   No, I don't play the banjo anymore. "I play guitar..., and sometimes I also play the fool! [9]".

Stue   Is that all?

John   No, I'm actually a singer and I play lead guitar, as they say, rhythm guitar.

Stue   Well, so there's room for a bass player.

John   Yeah. So you're coming to the audition?

Stue   Agree.

They split up.

---

[9] John's famous line.

Scene 9 - Pete Best

The Stage is a shimmering mix of the four legendary venues John has frequented: an imagined fusion of the Casbah, the Cavern, the Indra and the Kaiserkeller in Hamburg.

It allows us to get to know drummer Pete Best and to see behind the scenes, life "behind the scenes" when the Group, still maturing before becoming the Beatles, let loose between two concerts.

The set is an assembly of parts of the four venues, using the creativity and imagination of the set designer.

This setting requires the presence of musical instruments such as drums, guitars, piano and Vox amps.

The actors do not perform a show. Musically, they tap during the 'break' between two 'performances'. The fans are not present.

However, this scene can be the occasion for an unexpected 'musical moment'.

John is slumped over the piano, asleep.

Pete slowly puts the guitars away and puts them back on their stands.

Pete Best, son of Mona Best, patron of the Casbah in Liverpool, is a drummer.

As he walks past, he sits down at the drums and plays a few bars that wake John up.

John   (ironically) Are you all right, Indian?

Pete   Wait, I'm going to put on my feathered hat!

John   But   no, not that Indian! The other Indian! By
          the way, I never asked you: where were you
          born? Not in Liverpool?

Pete   Not in Hamburg or Kansas City either, but in
          Madras.

John   (sarcastically) Is that where you learned to dress?
          (He criticizes his very rock'n'roll look). But
          you've got the banana!

Pete   Yes, so what?

John   And that leather jacket that never leaves your
          shoulders, always very Rock!

Pete   Well, yeah. That's where we come from, isn't it?

John   Partly, but nowadays we dress differently! All
          the same, it's more stylish! Didn't your mother
          tell you that when we were in the Casbah? And
          we don't only play Rock, we prefer "my" songs,
          "x'cuse-me", the songs I compose with Paul and
          the others.

Pete   Well, it's ok to me.

John   Where are the others?

Pete   Stue is with his new girlfriend Astrid Kirchherr
          and her boyfriend, Klaus Voormann.

John   And Paul?

Pete   He drinks his beer. He sleeps in our lazarette by
         the toilet. He's exhausted, but he doesn't want to
         take any more Prellies.

John   I'm surprised, with the number of gigs we're
         asked to do every night in front of this audience
         of losers and phonies!

Pete   You bet your ass! You don't do anything to calm
         them down by calling them Nazis.

John   Have you seen how excited they get with "Hully
         Gully"?

Pete   Fucking right, it rocks every time you play it!
         They fight and they break everything.

John   And when you want to make them dance all
         night, you play "What I'd Say", it works every
         time!

Pete   Yeah, they don't stop!

John   But wait! I've got another thing going on right
         now! (He takes his electric guitar, plugs it in and
         starts playing).

For the staging, it depends: one can play and sing
dubbing or live, however the drums should be live.
This stage would benefit from a "total" show part with a
drummer, singer-guitarist who would encourage the
audience to participate by clapping their hands for

example. A sort of jam session to create an unexpected atmosphere.
The song played (to choose from some suggestions like "Roll Over Beethoven", "Johnny B. Goode", "Dizzy Miss Lizzy", "Lucille") is the following:
"Long Tall Sally'. It's obviously a catchy rock'n'roll tune.

Pete   (ends with a little solo).

John   (finishes and bows, then they leave the stage).

Scene 10 - Hamburg

Allan Williams, owner of the Jacaranda in Liverpool, became the manager of the first Beatles and proposed them to Bruno Koschmider, owner of the Indra and the Kaiserkeller in Hamburg.
Having returned from a tour in Scotland, they set off for the Hanseatic city, ready to play 'all out'.

A cabinet, a sort of vertical cupboard in a corner. An elongated loudspeaker of the Vox brand. Photos of the Beatles from the time, taken by Astrid Kirchherr, are hung on wires in various places on the stage. The lighting is subdued, except for a few spotlights directed at the photos. A nightclub atmosphere.

(John does not admit that Stu wants to get engaged to Astrid Kirchherr, a photographer and friend of Klaus Voormann.)

John   Klaus, I'd like to get something to eat: I'm starving.

Klaus   Speaking of eating, did you know that the word hamburger comes from here, from this city where you are?

John   Hamburg?

Klaus   Yes, Hamburg! (He pronounces it in German)

John   No; we English, are more like fish and chips. When we're not rationed...

Klaus   ...yes, it was a dirty war...on both sides...Afterwards, you see, people like us became friends, real friends.

John   Yes, the hamburger is more for those hungry Yankees.

Klaus   One day you may go to America, to the USA, with your future fame.

John   Yes, I hope so.

Klaus   I believe in it.

John   So do I.

Klaus sits on a speaker, John stands.
Music: short extract from 'I'm a Jealous Guy'.

John   (changing the subject) Your girlfriend, Astrid Kirchherr, the photographer, is she dating someone else now?

Klaus   Apparently.

John   And you don't care?

Klaus   That's the way it is, there's nothing I can do about it!

John   (in a bad mood) I told you I wanted her to go out with me last night and she and I would go to the cinema together!

Klaus   I don't have to tell her what to do and who to date, and neither do you. She's old enough to know what she wants and decide for herself.

John   (furious, approaches the cupboard and kicks and punches it). This is not what I fucking wanted! You knew I liked her and wanted to go out with her. (He calms down a bit). She's so hot, your blonde girlfriend! She was for me.

Klaus   Yes, but she decided otherwise. She fell for your friend Sutcliffe, the bass player, who, it must be said, is cute.

John   Maybe he's very attractive, but I don't care about that. It wasn't his job! He was supposed to play bass in my band and that's it!

Klaus   But love decided otherwise.

John   Love? Are you taking the piss? Where do you
          see love? It's just sex, yes. Full stop.

Klaus   You say that because you are driven by jealousy
          and it makes you angry.

John   According to you, am I jealous of him...or her?
          (Small wry smile).

Klaus   That's another matter! You should calm down
          and stop taking those "prellies"; you're taking
          too many of them and it's not working for you.

John   You, you don't have to tell me what to do either.
          And these Preludine pills help us to keep up
          with all those diabolical and frantic appearances
          we have to make on stage at a hellish pace, you
          know that! Here, we work with all kinds of pick-
          me-ups, we drink, we fight sometimes, we drink
          again, we collapse and we fall asleep on stage.
          For a prelude, it's a famous prelude... and it lasts
          a long time!

Klaus   And when you're not too exhausted, you still go
          out with me in the early morning so I can show
          you some typical Hamburg places and take your
          mind off things.

John   Yeah, that's about right. You're my buddy.

Klaus   So, you calm down and say to yourself that "the
          hell with it". You leave them alone.

John   We'll see...

Klaus   By the way, we know that you have already had
         a fight with Stue.

John   We were drunk.

Klaus   Maybe, but anyway you fight with everyone.

John   We   were drunk. Not with everyone.

Klaus   Let's say, well, almost.

John   All right, come on! Enough talk. Come on, take
         me for a drink.

Klaus   Let's go. In Hamburg, there are as many girls as
         you want in this neighbourhood. If you don't
         find one here, you won't find one anywhere else!

(They leave happily).

A church, chapel or temple setting. Basic, simplified.
An illuminated montage of an ogival (gothic) stained glass window, lit from behind.
A pulpit of truth and a Priest perched on it for a sermon.
Four characters seen from behind, with mop top hair and grey suits, listening to the priest.
Remember that Paul and George had a Catholic upbringing, and that John and Ringo were of the Anglican faith.

The priest   My dear Sisters, my dear Brothers; dear parishioners.

Today we welcome back our four friends John, George, Paul and Richard who are doing us the great honour of spending a little time with us in our beautiful Parish of St Peter's.

I am delighted to welcome them. An opportunity to wish them all the best for their future as musicians and stars of the modern show business.

But it is also an opportunity to remind ourselves how difficult and complicated it is to resist temptation. To the Temptations of this world, which draw us every day towards new traps, the throes of existence and, if we are not watchful, the depths of our Civilisation. Let us be vigilant, dear parishioners, so that we do not fall into all these traps that the Devil sets for us to stagger, fall, and perhaps lose us! Let us remember how important it is to fight, to resist.

My children, my four friends, do not succumb to Blasphemy! Do not let yourselves be tempted and subjugated by all that this modern world offers us to divert us from the right path: let us not allow drugs to creep into our lives; adultery to interfere with our marriage; repeated infidelity to pervert us; let us not give in to divorce, alcohol, other equally harmful substances, brawls and fights, sex and depravity; pagan rituals and distant religions, prohibitions of all kinds, blasphemy claiming that we are more famous than our Lord Jesus Christ[10].

(He breathes for a moment).

All this is the work of the Evil One and is only meant to divert us from the right path. The Devil is everywhere: think of St George!

(He gets more and more excited).

My Sisters, My Brothers, today's society is too permissive; let us not be tempted by ease, by all kinds of cravings offered to us by excessive consumption. Let us know how to show moderation today. In this materialistic world, let us fight by showing more Love and Spirituality.

---

[10] Allusion to John's sentence.

(He breathes again).

> Brothers John, George, Paul and Richard, whether it is us, your Catholic or Anglican Brothers, we will always be by your side to help and support you. We are so pleased and flattered that the four of you have come to spend a moment of meditation with your loved ones, (His pathos increases one last time) those whom you knew and loved when you were younger. Thank you! May the Peace of the Lord be with you always!

(The Four get up and leave. A voice is heard, probably John's)

We got a good kick out of that one!

Scene 12 - With Elvis Presley

Mythical appearance (for John at least) of Elvis on in a stage costume and with his guitar.

Elvis   (starts "Heartbreak Hotel", and then stops). (To John) So you like it?

John   (sitting as if in a theatre) Well yes, it was this song that convinced me to play rock. It drove me crazy to hear it. And I thought: I've always wanted to do this!

Elvis   I kind of sparked your vocation then?

John   You've drawn my attention to this new music, Rock'n roll.

Elvis   (humorously) Yeah, we were a bit early...

John   Of course, but there were other rockers who inspired me. And then, later, with the Beatles, I did what you did!

Elvis   Did you? Did you follow me?

John   Yeah. In America, your nice country, we wanted to go on the Ed Sullivan show. A stepping stone of sorts!

Elvis   And did it work?

John   You bet, it launched several of our songs into the UK charts, but more significantly into the US hits.

Elvis   Yeah ! (Not a little proud) the American market! (He makes a big gesture) The biggest in the world! That's why they said the English are invading the United States...

John   For my promotion, and pushing our Manager a bit, Brian Epstein, I went further and used other stepping stones, but keep that for you!

Elvis   What kind?

John   I was on Sunday Night at the London Palladium where I met Alma Cogan.

Elvis   Yes, indeed, you are clever. You've been to as many shows as possible, and like me, you've been in movies too. That's a good point!

John   Except that in this case, I fell on a bone!

Elvis   Which one is it?

John   We fell in love.

Elvis   Alma and you?

John   Yes.

Elvis   Well, it happens.

John   Except that Cynthia, my wife, found out.

Elvis   Aï!

John   And she said that Alma was probably my real 'first love'.

Elvis   This girl?

John   Yes, Alma.

Elvis   How did it go?

John   I had a hard time catching up, I can tell you. I've been wary ever since.

Elvis   Girls, they drive us crazy!

John   Yes, except the fans! They are too much. They get hysterical and you can't even hear yourself singing on stage. I'm fed up with it.

Elvis   Don't worry, I had the same thing.

John   But you are the King!

Elvis   So what?

John   In the US, you should be the President. The Queen is at home, in my country.

Elvis   Maybe. Anyway, I've never been bothered by all those screaming chicks and their noise. On the contrary, I find it very amusing and flattering.

John   Well, I don't! I find it extremely disturbing and insulting to our music. Did you see our show? Our second show at the Shea Stadium in Flushing Meadows. The worst show ever! No respect for our music, just letting off steam, screaming, yelling. I called it a "Tribal Rite".

(video)

At Candle Stick Park, they locked us up on stage in the middle of the stadium behind gates, like animals in a Zoo. They transported us in an armoured van!...

Elvis   ...like "small change"! Yet you are worth much more!

John   After that, there was Manila, where we were attacked because we refused Mrs Marco's invitation. Then the USA again, with threats, following my statement on Christianity. Fed up!

Elvis   You've just gone crazy, mate, that's all! It's like your ego took a hit. And the other members of your group followed, apparently.

John   You bet! I sing to be heard! Not the other way round! From now on, I'm going to hide out in the studio. With George Martin. That'll calm me down and give free rein to my creativity, my originality. That's what music is all about, inventing a completely personal style! And new! (He continues) You know what I said to an insidious journalist who asked me if I didn't mind not hearing my music when we were singing in public with all that shouting?

Elvis   No.

John   (facetiously) I said, "It doesn't matter, I have the records at home! ».

Elvis   (Elvis smiled) You're a happy iconoclast. You don't like the stage anymore, that feeling of being on stage and dominating the crowd?

John   (frustrated) I'm done! Success and fame don't excite us like they used to!

Elvis   You seemed to be having a good time, I thought.

John   Have fun, yes, but no longer suffer!

Elvis   Yet you are the Star! I heard you met Cassius Clay, aka Muhammad Ali, and he asked you how it felt to be a Star.

John   I replied: "It's simple: the more real you are, the more unreal the World will become".

Elvis   Nice answer!

John   Thank you, but in truth, the real star, the showman is you!

Elvis   You tried to copy me, didn't you?

John   Yes, in part.

Elvis   My wiggle, the leather...

John   Yes, but that's all over. Plus, with the suits that Brian is forcing on us!

Elvis   (ironic) What, you don't like it?

John   (shy) Not my style!

Elvis   Yet it created your style, and at first you agreed.

John   Yes, that's right. Everything that makes us
          special and original: the mop top haircut, the
          suit and tie, the boots, the simple guitars, the
          creativity, the tenacity, the folk music and later
          the rock, the ten thousand hours of performing,
          the personal compositions, doing the backing
          vocals ourselves and singing with four people, a
          determined manager, a good arranger, a
          professional four-track set-up.
          Our trademark, so to speak!

Elvis   Yes, you don't get there without working. It is
          well deserved.

(Elvis comes out. We hear the shouts of the crowd
waiting for him outside).

Scene 13 - Freud's house

John at the Psychotherapist.
Penumbra. John is lying on the famous couch.
A figure that looks an awful lot like Sigmund Freud sits
behind him, a small light illuminating his notes attached

on a clipboard. Strangely, Freud wears the same round glasses as John.

Freud   So, tell me what you were doing with this Dr. Arthur Janov and his primal therapy.

John   (bluntly) Scream!

Freud   Shout?

John   Yes, shout.

Freud   How is that?

John   (the line should try to achieve a comic effect to make the audience laugh) Like this (He shouts in the manner of his records with Yoko).

Freud   Yes, uh..., okay, okay... I see, or rather, I hear. And that's it?

John   Yes. Primal.

Freud   Well, I see.

John   I have come for your help.

Freud   Why is this so?

John   Too many problems in my life.

Freud   Well, all right. I can help you, if at least you agree and if you put your mind to it.

John   I hear you.

Freud   And these cries, tell me, do they remind you of
          anything?

John   Yes, it is.

Freud   What does this mean to you?

John   (ironic) My fans!

Freud   Yes, I see. But you're going a bit far, perhaps.
          Anything else?

John   Yes, it is.

Freud   I am listening.

John   My mother... and my Aunt.

Freud   And your trip to India, to the Guru Maharishi
          Mahesh Yogi, didn't help?

John   Yes, but not quite.

Freud   Why is this so?

John   Because me and my mates finally realised that he
          was laughing at us, that he was taking the piss
          out of us.

Freud   Really?

John   Yes, with Mia Farrow's daughter. I actually wrote a song about it, called Dear Prudence.

Freud   And what about LSD?

John   I've used it. It helped me to compose sometimes. Some of the lyrics are a bit convoluted for example.

Freud   And India?

John   Apart from the discomfort with the guru, we composed a lot on the spot.

Freud   What about heroin?

John   It came later. I went to rehab.

Freud   Did the absence of a father generate anxieties in you?

John   Yes, certainly. But my compositions help me to exorcise all that.

Freud   Who was your worst enemy? Your father?

John   No.

Freud   Your mother?

John   No.

Freud   Your Aunt Mimi?

John   No. (After a moment's reflection) Paul!

Freud   Aren't you exaggerating? Rather than a latent war, wasn't it, to call it like that, a healthy emulation? You created wonderful things together, you were the best creative pairing that ever existed in this music. In India you were very inventive again, very prolific; up to fifty songs, go figure, between you two! Not to mention the other two guys.

John   Yes, in fact, it was good to get a change of scenery, and especially to get away from all the pressure of having to "perform" all the time.

Freud   Do you like to settle scores?

John   It depends.

Freud   In your youth, did you witness any violent scenes that would have revolted you?

John   I don't think so.

Freud   So your revolt comes from elsewhere... You know the phrase: "Man is his own worst enemy"?

John   Yes, I think about it sometimes.

Freud   How can we be good to others if we are not
         good to ourselves?

John   I'm having trouble.

Freud   Are you ready to question yourself?

John   I have to think about it.

Freud   Aren't you your own worst enemy?

John   I don't know...maybe.

Freud   Are you afraid of abandonment? Do you always
         run to the arms of a woman? Are you attracted
         to opposites or are you running away from
         yourself?

John   I am looking for an image.

Freud   Can you express who you are?

John   Probably in my songs.

Freud   Aren't you in a fight with the whole world?

John   (speaking derisively of himself) John the
         extravagant! A restless agitator!

Freud   (completing as if nothing had happened) Beauty
         is often born from mire... And your teachers, did
         they find you surly?

John   (bravado) They didn't want to recognise my genius.

Freud   What does money mean to you?

John   Not a lot!

Freud   You talk about it a lot in your songs anyway: Money, Taxman, Baby You Are a Richman, You Never Give Me Your Money, Can't Buy Me Love.

John   A reward for my efforts perhaps?

Freud   Have you ever said thank you to someone?

John   I don't know. (He changes his mind) Oh yes! To my audience.

Freud   And you know why?

John   Yes, because it gave me back my dignity.

Freud   Because your public recognised you! You needed to be recognised. That's the whole story. Your story! And every time this truth escaped you, you changed course, you tried something else, still until today.

John   What a frustration! Singing to be heard, and then not being heard. That was my search.

Freud   You have to recognise one thing: it is this research that has always underpinned, sustained your creativity. That's why you became John Lennon!

John   It's getting better all the time!...

Freud   Finally, you are right. You are right to say that your Fans don't listen to you any more, that they vampire you, they destroy you! You were right when you said that it was "a fucking tribal rite". By giving free rein to their desire to free themselves, to let go and to let off steam, they project their fantasies, their ego and their desire for freedom onto you. You become their voodoo doll for an irreversible exorcism. They inject all their frustrations into you and unload them on you. You become their totem, their imago. And when they leave, there is nothing left but ashes! You no longer exist. Your instinct, and above all your intuition, has explained this to you.

John   At least, you are right, I experienced it that way.

Freud   Do you want to add anything else?

John   I don't think anymore. I am drained.

Freud   (curiously insists) Have you really said everything?

John   Yes.

Freud   Thanks to this, having now reached this stage, you no longer need me. You have probably found the alter-ego.

John   Is it over?

Freud   Yes, thank you. You may leave.

John   (gets up, puts on his coat and leaves the office).

Freud   (after a moment, he gets up and goes to open the back door) You may enter!

A man appears through that door opposite the exit the singer has just taken. (This man will be later recognised as the FBI agent who will interrogate John).

Agent   So, were you able to get anything out of it?

Freud   There is nothing pathological about it. Childhood needs have not been met, which sometimes leads to overestimation, sometimes to underestimation, with plenty of resentment.

Agent   Yes, but that's your job as a shrink! Nothing else? Nothing that could be useful to us?

Freud   No, he didn't say anything!

Agent   Well, I know what to do.

Freud   What will you do?

Agent   Bugging him!

Freud   Nothing but that?

Agent   Order of President Nixon!

Freud   (says nothing)

Agent   And if he doesn't calm down, he will be
         expelled!

He leaves the room quickly.

Scene 14 - With Johnny

John and Johnny share a common fate: they are both
"fatherless". If you look deep enough, you'll find a lot in
common with these two men. But let's leave the details.

The TV set of a famous variety show.
Johnny Hallyday on stage, singing a Beatles song: "Got to
Get You into My Life".

The Presenter   Ladies and gentlemen, Johnny Halliday!
                 (Let's hear it for the audience).

The Presenter   Johnny, Johnny, come and have a seat
                 here next to me!

The Presenter	Johnny, so, how does it feel to revisit your repertoire and perform a Beatles song?
Johnny	(Johnny's speech is deliberately caricatured) Oh, I want, my nephew!
The Presenter	Yes, well. But you owe a lot of your success to them.
Johnny	Well, no, not really. Not quite.
The Presenter	Explain.
Johnny	Well, to tell you the truth, I was more of a rock and roll guy at first.
The Presenter	A bit like John, actually?
Johnny	Yes. But then things changed. There was the Yéyé wave, the Twist, the legendary broadcast and magazine "Salut les Copains".
The Presenter	You haven't followed the Beatles' career?
Johnny	No, I went my own way. Always on stage!
The Presenter	Like them.

Johnny	At first, yes, but not afterwards. I remain a "showman". They went to work in studio.
The Presenter	You now performed one of the four Beatles songs in your repertoire: "Got to Get You into My Life". Your friend Dick Rivers also performed one of their songs "Things We Said Today"-"Ces mots qu'on oublie un jour".
Johnny	He was not the only one, a lot of people did!
The Presenter	Certainly! Only for that song, there were 73 singing versions and 27 instrumentals plus 3 adaptations!
Johnny	Simply crazy!
The Presenter	Absolutely, I agree! And rewarding! What were the other three songs of The Beatles in your repertoire?
Johnny	First there was "I Saw Her Standing There". Then "She's a Woman". And at last "Girl".
The Host	And finally, we heard: "Got to Get You into My Life". Did you feel they were close to you and to your success?

Johnny	I always wanted to be famous by imitating others. They were different; they were inspired, original and had fun creating!
The Animator	Meaning?
Johnny	I realised straight away that the Beatles 'style' was so original that it was inimitable: boots, mop top hair, suits, music... The Beatles stimulated many more than me. Of course there are the other three members of the band, but John is particularly brilliant and inventive musically. He was singularly innovative.
The Host	What else?
Johnny	The musical style is also inimitable. Their musical harmony is exceptional. The use of special instruments, for example:

Excerpts of music to be cut out and edited if possible to illustrate.

harmonica (Love Me Do); flute: (The Fool On the Hill); violins: (Yesterday); trumpet: (All You Need is Love); piano: (Lady Madonna); harp (She's Living Home); clapping (I Want to

Hold Your Hand); shouting (Roll Over Beethoven, Carol); etc.

Just think of the use of backing vocals, which they have always done alone, in two and three voices like in Twist and Shout.

The composition and lyrics, first borrowed, often from Rock, then elaborated by themselves; lyrics inspired by everyday life (A Day in the Life, Penny Lane); a disciplined drummer who never plays solos, (except in The End); generally very short songs, no longer than 2.5 minutes (except Her Majesty or Hey Jude); a short solo piece, the "bridge", usually by George, placed in the middle of the song (Something, While My Guitar); a bass that plays the melody rather than the supporting the rhythm (Being for the Benefit of Mr. Kite!); using the emerging technology of four-track recording and studio arrangements; an outstanding producer, musician, arranger, George Martin (piano solo in In My Life); Brian Epstein, a motivated Manager. Sound effects: I'm Only Sleeping (yawn); Good Morning (rooster); Revolution 9 (sounds); Sergeant Pepper (showroom); It's all too much, etc.

The Host	It's true, that's a lot! You did well to point this out and help us understand their music! And yours!
Johnny	With pleasure, my nephew. (He gets up and leaves the set).
The Host	Ladies and gentlemen, let's hear it for Johnny Hallyday!

Scene 15 - A Revolutionary or Protest John?

In this scene, we consider John's most representative songs of that time (Working Class Hero, Power to the People, Give Peace a Chance, Woman is the Nigger of the World, God...).

An apartment door on the garden side, an office door on the courtyard side; there is a desk and two chairs discreetly placed on the courtyard side.

A noisy intrusion at John's house. Two FBI detectives arrive and one of them knocks loudly on the door of the garden flat.

The Inspector	(speaking through the door) Mr Lennon?
John	Yes.
The Inspector	Sir (he insists) John Lennon?

John   (he answers through the door) Yes. What do you want?

The Inspector   We would like to interview you at the FBI premises in New York. This won't take long. Could you come with us, please?

John   What am I being accused of?

The Inspector   Nothing. We'll talk about it there if you like.

John   Good. I'll be right out. (He puts on a coat and goes out).

(They wait)

John   I'll follow you...

They hurriedly walk around the stage and immediately return to the other side; they open the door and find themselves in front of the desk on the courtyard side which had remained in the shadow. They sit down. One of the two FBI agents remains standing.
Spotlight a little blinding, but not in an "interrogative" way like in the movies.

The Inspector   Mr. Lennon, I am Inspector Cox and this is Agent Dipps. I'm going to ask you some questions about your application to the United States Immigration Service.

John   I'm listening. (Then he casually makes an insidious remark) Apparently it's getting a bit sticky...

The inspector   Mr. Lennon, as you know from having filled it out more than once, in America, I mean in the United States of America, there is no box on the application form to say that an applicant is without religion? You know that, don't you?

John   I have more than noticed.

The Inspector   Here in America, everyone has a religion. So what is yours?

John   I am a non-believer

The inspector   And?

John   And what?

The inspector   And so, as there is no such thing in our country, what did you declare?

John   I put Anglican I think, because that's where I come from.

The inspector   Right. In one of your songs, which can be considered public since you are a "public" man (he insists on the word), you say: "God is a "concept" by which we measure our pains".

John — So what?

The inspector — That implies a non-belief, don't you think?

John — I just say I don't believe in anyone but myself anymore.

The Inspector — It's a bit short, admit it. And it contradicts what you have just said.

John — This is not the Inquisition, is it?

The Inspector — Certainly not, nor a witch hunt! But you have to admit that it can be shocking.

John — (Does not answer).

The inspector — Let's get back to the matter at hand.

John — I'm waiting.

The Inspector — Let's talk about your activities on American soil, and more specifically about your political actions.

John — It seems to me that this is a right, a fundamental freedom.

The Inspector   Maybe, but it depends how far you can
                       go.

John   Really?

The inspector   ...Possession of cannabis... Residence
                       permit denied... The Nixon
                       Administration does not seem to
                       appreciate these complicated times...

John   I don't find it seditious.

The Inspector   When one demonstrates against the
                       Vietnam War, don't you think that's
                       against public authority?

John   Not basically!

The inspector   How do you call it?

John   Freedom of expression.

The Inspector   And by preventing thousands of
                       Americans from fulfilling their civic
                       obligations to their country?

John   (He says nothing)

The inspector   What do you call that? Agitation?
                       Dissent, protest?

John   (nothing)

The Inspector	A call to mutiny? Desertion? Do you know what sedition is? You can't go as far as a rebel uprising or worse, what the military call desertion.
John	It's not about that at all, I'm a peace activist.
The Inspector	Are you an activist?
John	I ask, along with thousands of others around the world, for peace. That we stop this bloody war where young people are being slaughtered and where we take away their possibility of living.
The Inspector	You do understand that this is not appreciated in these complicated times, coming from someone who is not an American citizen? President Nixon himself is concerned about the extent of this "protest".
John	I am English, that's right!
The Inspector	Let's turn to the Possession of Cannabis.
John	Unfortunate raid of your services for a few grams!
The inspector	Nevertheless, it is forbidden here!

John   I am not a trafficker or a dealer (he
                        suddenly thinks of his father).

The Inspector   Your left-wing buddies seem to enjoy
                        these illegal substances as much as you
                        do.

John   Just because you think left doesn't mean
                        you're a dissident.

The inspector   That's what we're trying to find out.

John   Our thinking is universal.

The Inspector   Maybe, but your actions, especially
                        against the war in Vietnam, are more,
                        how shall I say, "colourful"?

John   This is my vision and my commitment, I
                        want World Peace.

The Inspector   Mr Lennon, I ask you to answer the
                        following question truthfully: were you
                        ever like this when you were in
                        Liverpool?

John   (thinking). No, I don't think so.

The Inspector   Do you think your current wife was your
                        mentor?

John	Yoko has helped me a lot to see things clearly and I love her. I don't allow you to blame her and accuse her.
The Inspector	Did you know, for example, that in 1975, in a small country like Belgium where she went, she personally participated in a support evening for the newspaper "Pour", not to be named, which was described as extreme left-wing, in order to replenish its coffers following an extreme right-wing attack on[11] them?
John	She participated as an Avant-garde artist, I think.
The inspector	No doubt...
John	All this does not make me an activist!
The Inspector	That remains to be seen... In the same year you participated in a rally in Hyde Park, London. In '71 and '72 you had already made a big impact with your songs, especially "Sunday Bloody Sunday". And now it's much more serious. It was a rally in favour of the IRA, the Irish Liberation Army. Your grandfather was of Irish origin: his name was Ó Leannáin.

---

[11] Exhibition under the "SaltoArte" tent in 1975 on Place Flagey in Brussels.

John Lennon attends an unspecified rally in Hyde Park, London, England, 1975.

John	In this demonstration I spoke in favour of Irish independence.
The Inspector	Against the interests of your own country?
John	Freedom knows no boundaries!
The inspector	To the point of funding them?
John	I know the editor of their newspaper, the Red Mole, if that's what you mean?
The inspector	Yes, that's exactly what it is, and it's not innocent. For us, the FBI, and our British colleagues, this is a very serious matter!

John	I'm more moderate than that and I'm mellowing out.
The inspector	We are obliged to consider all this following your immigration application.
John	I understand.
The inspector	You don't own a gun, I suppose?
John	No.
The Inspector	Are you an anti-militarist?
John	You could say that.
The inspector	Here in America you can have a gun, it's not forbidden. You might need it one day to defend yourself... (Curious premonitory words?)
John	I don't understand...
The Inspector	Well, sir, that's all for now. I'll let you go.
John	(ironically, as he stands up) Hello...Goodbye!
The inspector	(gets up to conclude the interview) You know, I listen to your songs too!
John	(moving towards the door) Surely this will help, then…

The second officer follows them and goes out with them.

The lights go out, as if to announce the beginning of the next dramatic scene. The room and the stage remain in darkness and silence for a moment.

Scene 16 - Murder

A New York street along Central Park. A New York building portico on the courtyard side.
John returns from the "Record Plant", the famous recording studio in New York.
He comes from the garden side and goes to the courtyard side. A man standing on the courtyard porch comes towards him. They meet in the middle of the stage. The man has a book out of his pocket. He asks John:

Chapman   John, would you autograph these records for me, please? (He hands him two copies of "Double Fantasy").

John   Certainly. (He stops and signs. Then resumes walking towards the courtyard).

Chapman   (he ostensibly throws the discs away, then pulls out a revolver). (He shoots John five times in the back, who collapses, struck down). (The explosions are very loud, deafening).

John   (Yelling) "Help me. Someone shot me"!

The scene is plunged into darkness, like a nightmare. Police and ambulance sirens can be heard. Blue lights. Then someone asks:

Voice   (the policeman) Are you John Lennon?

Switching off all lights.

Scene 17 - J.D. Salinger appears in the cell

The murderer Mark David Chapman is in prison.
On stage, Salinger is alone, sitting in an armchair.
We witness an imaginary dialogue between the writer J.D. Salinger and the assassin Mark David Chapman.

Salinger   (with American accent) I am Jerome David Salinger. (We see his portrait on a slide). I am an American writer. I have written many short stories, published in newspapers in my country. I also wrote the novel "The Catcher in the Rye", which people say has inspired you for your murder, Mark Chapman. But is it really true?

There is obviously no answer from Mark Chapman.

Salinger   As a writer, I've kept my strange temper and you may have guessed it? I am like that. The war has left its mark on me. I am Jewish. In the Second World War, I volunteered to fight in Normandy against the Nazis. I landed on Utah Beach on D-Day. I fought in some tough battles: the so-called Battle of the Bulge in Belgium and the Battle of the Hürtgen Forest further on in Germany. These battles lasted more than three months.
I then joined the US Intelligence Service to inform our troops of anything that would help us to win the war and then, just after the war, to denazify Germany.
I am motivated, committed!
But the war traumatized me heavily, as you can imagine! Especially when I entered the concentration camp, Kaufering IV, a sub-camp of Dachau.
After all these horrors, I had to be hospitalised for "combat stress reaction". It's a psychic disorder. You can imagine!
It was very traumatic for me. It left an emotional mark on me, you can understand.
This too probably explains the character I created in the novel "The Catcher in the Rye", Holden Caulfield. He certainly looks like me, but only in part. He hasn't experienced all the horrors and suffering I have. He's the son of a fancy lawyer. A

simple American teenager of sixteen, lost in his city of New York, in the middle of winter, kicked out of school because he doesn't like school (maybe because he can't fit in). He is also a victim of his impulses. On the other hand, he has a little sister, Phoebe, whom he adores. He has not lived through the War. He hasn't been through what I have!

One might wonder, therefore, when reading my book, whether this kid's malaise is comparable to mine and to that of the whole generation that lived through the immediate post-war period, like John Lennon for example. My teenager is disillusioned, perhaps even disoriented and idle, as John and his friends probably were after the war.

But, in any case, it is not comparable at all in my opinion! You have to put things in their place!

One deprivation is not the other! And we are living much better today! John was able to react and you know what happened. He had a glorious planetary success.

My hero is Holden Caulfield, he is like that. He's depressed. He's a loser, in a way. You identified with him, for some of his aspects, notably his psychotic accident. That's just a detail. You're not Holden Caulfield! You're Mark Chapman; you may be jealous, angry and disappointed. You don't have my experience at all. You don't have my hero's background either. You may share some secondary similarities with him: you failed at school, you were depressed and even tried to kill yourself with your car's exhaust fumes, but it didn't work! You failed miserably! Well, well, well! Your character is suddenly starting to interest me!

John, on the other hand, is not as you describe him. He is not disappointing. He didn't let go or abandon anyone. On the contrary, he always wanted to make amends. It was not because he was rich that he gave up his convictions. On the contrary, he was still 'campaigning' (if you can use that expression) for world peace when you say you were disappointed. On the other hand, what "annoyed" you was also his lack of respect for Jesus and for God. That famous sentence that went round the world, "Today we are more popular than Jesus", which he later went back on. Perhaps you are confusing these two different motives? Where did you get these ideas of rebellion in your turn? Where does your rebellion come from? Are you a fanatic rather than a fan? Isn't John also like you? You have a lot in common. You're not going to end the life of a world-famous music star because he questions things? Because his character is a protestor?

Or do you have other motives, outside of all this?

(He stops for a moment).

Now the curtain has fallen and you are alone with your mistake!

(He gets up slowly and leaves the stage).

The slamming of a prison door is heard.
The lights go out.

Scene 18 - The assassin Mark David Chapman

During the scene, some pictures are projected:
- John signing with Chapman
- Dumdums bullets
- A Charter Arms special 38 Undercover revolver

After the scene:
- The Strawberry Fields monument in New York Central Park
- People recalling
- Candles
- Paul
- George
- Ringo

Music: "I Want You (She's So Heavy)". This John's song is famous for the fact that when it was finished on 20 August 1969, the four Beatles were together for the very last time in the studio. (Happiness is a Warm Gun can also be played).

The Policeman   You stated that you killed John Lennon. Were you manipulated?

Chapman   Why do you ask?

The Policeman   It is said that you were in contact with spooks in Hawaii when you worked for the YMCA?

Chapman   I don't see where this is going.

The Policeman   You made consecutively two trips from Hawaii to USA to kill John Lennon. You must have been very motivated?

Chapman   I was anguished to miss him.

The Policeman   Did you plan the crime?

Chapman   Yes.

The Policeman   But this requires money!

The Policeman   No problem, I was working and my wife too.

The Policeman   Why did you use hollow-point bullets?

Chapman   To make sure you don't miss it!

The Policeman   Do you know the damage that this kind of projectile does?

Chapman   Yes, I am a former Security Officer.

The Policeman   What bothered you about the song "Imagine"?

Chapman   (humming) "Imagine no possessions, I wonder if you can, No need for greed or hunger

The Policeman   And that's all? You don't murder a man for his words, do you? Do you?

Chapman   I find it unbearable that he would say these words when he owns so much: apartments, yachts, art galleries, farms and properties in the countryside, and myself I live in a two-room flat...

The Policeman   ...and that's why...

Chapman   (interrupts) I admired him so much, he who sang peace... I was betrayed!

The Policeman   (addressing the officer who has remained standing) Send in the Doctor.

The Doctor enters. We recognize John's psychologist by his appearance and his round shaped glasses. He seems to be wearing a cape or some other garment that makes him intriguing.

The Doctor	(he sits down. He has his notebook with him). (He continues quickly) Why did you kill that man?
Chapman	He bothered me, his fame bothered me. I am more famous than he is!
The Doctor	(mumbles)...Sleazy, sleazy... (then loudly) Because you think you've done more than he has to become as famous as you think? Were you obsessed with fame and celebrity?
Chapman	Yes.
The Doctor	(mumbles again) Sordid, squalid... (to Chapman) Really? And what did you do?
Chapman	I killed John Lennon!
The Doctor	(changing his tone completely, in a very "shrink" style and in a very direct way, as if to surprise) What do the ducks in Central Park do in winter when their pond is frozen? (A question that recurs in the Salinger novel that Chapman was reading at the time of the murder: "The Catcher in the Rye").
Chapman	(equally unexpected) Quack quack!

The Doctor	(after a moment). Why were you reading this book while waiting for Mister Lennon?

Chapman	"The Catcher in the Rye? That's mine! It's mine! I like Salinger a lot!

The Policeman	We found this book, your book, after the murder. Now answer the Doctor.

Chapman	He's famous, I'm a fan. I got him to sign autographs.

The Policeman	That's not the question! Why were you reading this book?

The Doctor	(insisting) Why did you have Salinger's "A Catcher in the Rye" with you when you killed Mr John Lennon?

Chapman	(silence)

The Policeman	You said: "I'm sure the big part of me is Holden Caulfield, who is the main character in the book. The small part of me must be the devil".

Chapman	Give me "my" book. I will read you the passage where all is revealed! (He receives the book, opens it, flips through it to find the passage). (He reads):

"I keep picturing all these little kids playing some game in this big field of rye and all. Thousands of little kids, and nobody's around - nobody big, I mean - except me. And I'm standing on the edge of some crazy cliff. What I have to do, I have to catch everybody if they start to go over the cliff. I mean if they're running and they don't look where they're going, I have to come out from somewhere and catch them. That's all I'd do all day. I'd just be the catcher in the rye and all. I know it's crazy, but that's the only thing I'd really like to be. I know it's crazy".

(He closes the book and keeps it ostensibly on the table in front of him).

You see, I'm not crazy!

The Policeman ...and the Religion?

Chapman   I just wanted to shout out loud: "Who does he think he is, this Lennon, saying these things about God and heaven and the Beatles? ». Saying he doesn't believe in Jesus and stuff like that!

The Policeman That's not quite right. He talked about his own fame in relation to Jesus; he said "We're more popular than Jesus now", and then he later went back on those words.

Chapman   (silence).

The Doctor   Did your father take care of you a lot? Was he a present or an absent father?

Chapman   My father was in the US Air Force; I didn't see much of him; in fact, hardly any. He didn't take care of me and was abusive to my mother who was a nurse. I was afraid of him; he had no love for me, he was not interested in me. I even ran away at one point.

The Policeman   And like Holden, your hero, you've skipped school!

Chapman   When I was young...

The Policeman   ...a teenager like your hero.

Chapman   Yes.

The Policeman   On the other hand, like Holden, the protagonist of the novel, you were furious.

Chapman   Yes, but I told you. I was angry at those people who don't do what they say!

The Policeman   That's fine. We'll leave it at that.

The scene is plunged into darkness.

We play 'The End' so that the audience understands that
it is over, then 'All you Need is Love'.

The End

"You don't stop playing when you get old; you get old when you stop playing".
John would certainly have approved of this quote from George Bernard Shaw, as he did not stop playing until the day he died.

"Life is all these faculties that I have given myself between the two worlds".

"The worst pain is not to be wanted, to find out that your parents do not want you the way you want them. When I was a child, I had moments when I didn't want to see the ugliness, didn't want to see that I wasn't wanted. That lack of love got into my eyes and into my mind.
I was never really wanted. The only reason I'm a star is because of my frustration. I wouldn't have had the strength to go through all this if I had been 'normal' "[12].

John Lennon.

---

[12] The Beatles Anthology published by Éditions du Seuil - 2000. In English, Chronicle Books - 2000. Copyright Apple Corps Ltd. 2000.

www.ingramcontent.com/pod-product-compliance
Lightning Source LLC
LaVergne TN
LVHW020052210726
843507LV00015B/1803